Events of
1960

News for every day of the year

I0441105

27 July: Troops from the Republic of
Ireland prepare to fly to the Congo
for their army's first engagement
since its formation in 1923.

By Hugh Morrison

MONTPELIER PUBLISHING

Published in Great Britain by Montpelier Publishing.
Printed and distributed by Amazon KDP.
This edition © 2019. All rights reserved.
ISBN: 9781098682309

January 1960

Friday 1: Cameroon becomes independent of France.

Saturday 2: The highest temperature on record in Australia, 50.7 C (123.3F) is reached in at Oodnadatta, Western Australia.

Sunday 3: The first *CBS Sports Spectacular* is shown on US TV.

Monday 4: French novelist Albert Camus *(left)* dies in a car accident near the town of Villeneuve-la-Guyard. The manuscript of his last novel, *The First Man*, is found in the wreckage; it is finally published 35 years later.

Tuesday 5: Britain's Prime Minister Harold Macmillan begins a six week tour of Britain's current and former African colonies.

Wednesday 6: Mr Eugene Barnes, 45, becomes the first person to be saved by the new technique of CPR (cardiopulmonary resuscitation) carried out by Dr Henry Thomas at John Hopkins University Hospital in Baltimore, Maryland.

Thursday 7: The USA tests the first Polaris nuclear missile using its own internal guidance system. President Eisenhower describes the weapons as 'one of our most effective sentinels for peace.'

Friday 8: Former US Marine Lee Harvey Oswald defects to the USSR. He returns in 1962 and is charged in 1963 with the assassination of President John F Kennedy.

Saturday 9: President Nasser officially inaugurates construction of the Aswan Dam in Egypt.

Sunday 10: Brian Cowen, Prime Minister of the Republic of Ireland 2008-11 is born in Clara, County Offaly.

January 1960

Monday 11: One of America's most prolific serial killers, Henry Lee Lucas, claims his first victim when he murders his mother in Tecumseh, Michigan. He goes on to confess to 600 slayings, eventually being convicted of 11.

Tuesday 12: *Scent of Mystery* is released in the USA. It is the first film to be shown in 'Smell-o-Vision', with various scents wafted through the cinema ventilation system.

Wednesday 13: 'Operation Zapata', the covert operation by the US government to overthrow Cuban revolutionary Fidel Castro, is launched.

Thursday 14: The Reserve Bank of Australia goes into operation.

Friday 15: The Soviet Union agrees to reduce its armed forces by nearly one third. Premier Kruschev announces that a large army is no longer required and asks for resources to be diverted into nuclear weapons.

Nobusuke Kishi.

Saturday 16: Riots break out in Tokyo as left-wing protestors demonstrate against Prime Minister Nobusuke Kishi travelling to the US to forge closer links via a joint defence treaty.

Sunday 17: It is announced that US President Dwight D. Eisenhower will undertake a ten-day tour of the USSR in June. The visit never takes place due to the U2 spyplane incident in May.

Dwight D Eisenhower.

January 1960

Monday 18: All 50 people on board perish when Capital Airlines Flight 20 crashes near Holdcroft, Virginia.

Tuesday 19: The Treaty of Mutual Cooperation and Security between the United States and Japan is signed in Washington.

Wednesday 20: The USSR successfully launches the first intercontinental ballistic missile (ICBM) demonstrating a range of over 7,000 miles.

Thursday 21: The rhesus monkey 'Miss Sam' is launched into space from Wallops Island, Virginia, as part of tests for the launch of the USA's first man in space.

Friday 22: Singer Michael Hutchence of INXS is born in Sydney, Australia (died 1997).

Saturday 23: Explorer Jacques Piccard and the US Navy's Lieutenant Don Walsh make a record descent of over seven miles in the bathyscaphe *Trieste* to the bottom of the Mariana Trench.

Sunday 24: In a protest over plans for independence, Europeans in the French colony of Algeria seal off parts of the capital Algiers.

The bathyscaphe *Trieste*.

January 1960

Peter Sellers: star of *The Goon Show*.

Monday 25: British composer Rutland Boughton (*The Immortal Hour*) dies aged 82.

Tuesday 26: Pete Rozelle of the Los Angeles Rams becomes the USA's National Football League Commissioner.

Wednesday 27: A river of lava from the Kilauea Volcano in Hawaii destroys the village of Kapoho.

Thursday 28: BBC radio broadcasts the final episode of comedy series *The Goon Show* starring Peter Sellers, Spike Milligan and Harry Secombe.

Friday 29: France's President Charles de Gaulle appears on TV in his military uniform, announcing that the future of Algeria will be left to the Arab majority. French troops are sent to quell the European rebellion in Algiers.

Saturday 30: Indian economist JC Kumarappa, founder of 'Ghandian' economics, dies aged 68.

President Charles de Gaulle of France.

Sunday 31: 19 soldiers are killed in a skirmish between Syrian and Israeli forces at Tawfiq, Syria.

February 1960

Monday 1: The first 'sit in' protest against racial segregation occurs in the USA when four students in Greensboro, North Caroline, refuse to leave a whites-only Woolworth's lunch counter.

Statue of the Greensboro protestors.

Tuesday 2: In Brooklyn, NY, billiards player Mike Eufemia sets a world record by potting 625 consecutive balls without a miss.

Wednesday 3: Britain's Prime Minister Harold Macmillan makes his 'wind of change' speech to the South African parliament, telling them that white minority rule will end. On the same day the French senate votes to strip European settlers in Algeria of their political power.

British Prime Minister Harold Macmillan.

Thursday 4: Jordan offers citizenship to anyone who held Palestinian citizenship before 1948, excluding Jews.

Friday 5: Work begins on the CERN particle accelerator in Geneva, Switzerland.

Saturday 6: Rock and roll singer Jessie Belvin (*Earth Angel*) dies in a car accident aged 27, following a concert with Sam Cooke and Jackie Wilson.

Sunday 7: Actor James Spader (*Sex, Lies and Videotape*) is born in Boston, Massachusetts.

February 1960

Left: the crew of the missing USAF bomber *Lady Be Good* in 1943.

Monday 8: The Hollywood Walk of Fame is opened. Burt Lancaster and Ronald Colman are among the first stars to be included.

Tuesday 9: Adolf Coors III, chairman of the Coors brewery, is kidnapped near his home in Morrison, Colarado. He is later found dead; Joseph Corbett Jr is convicted of his murder.

Wednesday 10: Soviet Premier Nikita Kruschev begins a 24-day tour of south Asia.

Thursday 11: The wreck of the USAF B52 bomber *Lady Be Good*, which disappeared in 1943, is discovered in the Libyan desert. The bodies of the surviving crew are found 85 miles away, where they had walked until they ran out of water.

Friday 12: Laurens Hammond, inventor of the Hammond Organ, retires.

Saturday 13: France becomes the world's fourth nuclear power when it detonates its first atomic bomb in a test in the Sahara Desert.

Sunday 14: Field Marshall Muhammed Ayub Khan becomes President of Pakistan.

February 1960

Monday 15: A military stand-off occurs between Israel and Egypt as Egypt receives inaccurate reports of Israeli troops massing on its border; both sides are stood down in March.

Tuesday 16: The nuclear submarine USS *Triton* begins its round the world undersea voyage with a crew of 184 people; it ends 83 days later.

Wednesday 17: It is announced that a nuclear early warning system will be built on the Yorkshire Moors in the north of England.

Thursday 18: The 1960 Winter Olympics opens in Squaw Valley, California; bad weather keeps many spectators away.

Friday 19: Prince Andrew, Duke of York and third child of Queen Elizabeth II, is born in London. He is the first child to be born to a reigning British sovereign since 1857.

HRH Prince Andrew.

Saturday 20: British archaeologist Leonard Woolley, famous for his excavations at Ur in Iraq, dies aged 79.

Sunday 21: Conductor André Previn makes the first of 51 appearances at New York's Carnegie Hall, playing the *Piano Concerto in F* by George Gershwin.

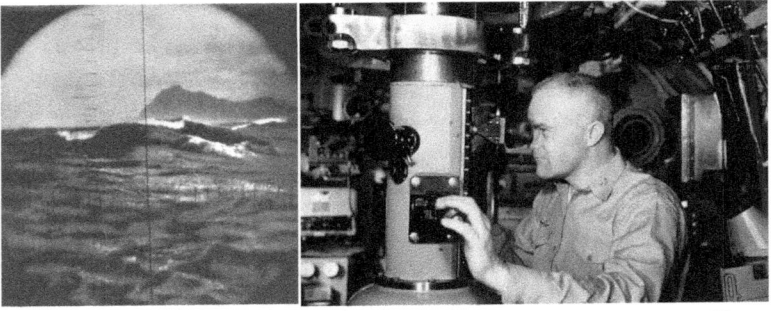

Capt Beach of the USS *Triton* and a periscope picture of Cape Horn.

February 1960

HRH Princess Margaret and Anthony Armstrong-Jones.

Monday 22: The most popular song of 1960, *Theme From a Summer Place* by Percy Faith and his Orchestra, reaches number one in the US.

Tuesday 23: Crown Prince Naruhito of Japan is born in Tokyo.

Wednesday 24: The USA tests its first intercontinental ballistic missile (ICBM) at Cape Canaveral. Previously, nuclear weapons were carried by manned aircraft or short range missiles.

Thursday 25: 61 people are killed when a US Navy aircraft and a Brazilian airliner collide over Rio de Janeiro.

Crown Prince Naruhito.

Friday 26: Princess Margaret, younger sister of Queen Elizabeth II, announces her engagement to photographer Antony Armstrong-Jones.

Saturday 27: Adriano Olivetti, founder of the Olivetti typewriter and office machines corporation, dies aged 58.

Sunday 28: The US ice hockey team wins the gold medal in the Winter Olympics by beating Czechoslovakia 9-4.

February/March 1960

Monday 29: At least 12,000 people are killed when an earthquake hits the city of Agadir in Morocco.

Tuesday 1: NASA begins research into exobiology to prevent the contamination of outer space by microbes from space vehicles.

Wednesday 2: German national airline Lufthansa launches its first jet liner, a Boeing 707.

Lucille Ball and Desi Arnaz.

Thursday 3: Comedienne Lucille Ball announces her divorce from on-screen and real-life husband, Desi Arnaz, three weeks after filming the final episode of their show, *I Love Lucy.*

Friday 4: 76 people are killed when a French cargo ship carrying 70 tons of munitions explodes in Havana harbour, Cuba.

Saturday 5: Elvis Presley is honourably discharged from the US army after two years of military service, where he reached the rank of Staff Sergeant. He remains a reservist until 1964.

Staff Sergeant Elvis Presley.

Sunday 6: US President Eisenhower announces that 3,500 American troops will be posted to South Vietnam.

March 1960

Monday 7: US writers' union The Screen Actors' Guild calls a strike for the first time in its history, halting the filming of eight major motion pictures.

Pioneer V.

Tuesday 8: Senator John F Kennedy wins the New Hampshire Primary election on the Democrat ticket.

Wednesday 9: Regular kidney dialysis becomes possible with the invention of the Scribner Shunt, a tube which connects arteries to veins.

Thursday 10: The first mitral heart valve replacement operations are carried out; the first patient dies 60 hours later but a second patient survives for 30 years.

Prince Constantine of Lesotho.

Friday 11: *Pioneer V* is launched from Cape Canaveral; it is the first man made object to be launched into solar (as opposed to Earth) orbit.

Saturday 12: Prince Constantine Bereng Seeiso, later King Moshoeshoe II of Lesotho, becomes Paramount Chief of the British colony of Basutoland.

Sunday 13: A total lunar eclipse enables the first infrared scans of the moon's surface, which identify 'hot spots' in the Tycho Crater.

March 1960

Monday 14: The Chancellor of West Germany, Konrad Adenauer, becomes the first German leader to meet an Israeli head of state, David Ben Gurion, during negotiations in New York.

Tuesday 15: 389 black protestors are arrested in Orangeburg, South Carolina, following a protest against segregated lunch counters.

Wednesday 16: The bodies of three women are found in Starved Rock State Park in Illinois; a park employee, Chester Weger, is later convicted of their murder.

Thursday 17: President Eisenhower authorizes the CIA to train and equip Cuban exiles in order to overthrow the Castro regime.

Friday 18: The 'Snark' nuclear missile is introduced in the USA; it is declared obsolete just 15 months later after the introduction of ICBMs (Intercontinental Ballistic Missiles).

A 'Snark' missile is launched.

Saturday 19: A portion of the restored Great Wall of China is opened to visitors.

Sunday 20: The Governor of Florida, Leroy Collins, previously thought to be in favour of racial segregation, announces on TV that he supports the recent lunch counter protests, adding 'we can never stop Americans from struggling to be free.'

March 1960

Monday 21: 69 protesters are killed in the Sharpeville Massacre, when police fire on a crowd in the black township of Sharpeville, South Africa.

Tuesday 22: The first laser, produced by Bell Laboratories, receives its US patent.

Wednesday 23: Marty Dalton, an inmate of the Rhode Island State Prison, dies aged 91 after serving 63 years imprisonment for murder, one of the longest terms served in US history.

Thursday 24: German singer Gabrielle Kerner, better known as Nena (*99 Luftballons*) is born in Hagen, West Germany.

Friday 25: The severed head of Oliver Cromwell, Lord Protector of England, is buried in an undisclosed location at his old college, Sidney Sussex, Cambridge, England, after being in private hands since the 17th century.

Saturday 26: X-ray research pioneer Dr Emil Herman Grubbe dies aged 85. He was the first person to be injured by radiation.

Sunday 27: The last regular steam train passenger service in the USA ends, between Detroit and Durand, Michigan.

Near to this place was buried on 25 March 1060 the head of **OLIVER CROMWELL** Lord Protector of the Commonwealth of England, Scotland & Ireland, Fellow Commoner of this College 1616

Cromwell and his memorial plaque. Cromwell died of natural causes but his body was exhumed and beheaded in 1661.

March/April 1960

Monday 28: US Congressman Russell V Mack collapses and dies from a cerebral haemorrhage during a vote in the House of Representatives.

Tuesday 29: Dr Melvin Cook is awarded a patent for the first water-based explosive, far safer than dynamite in industrial applications.

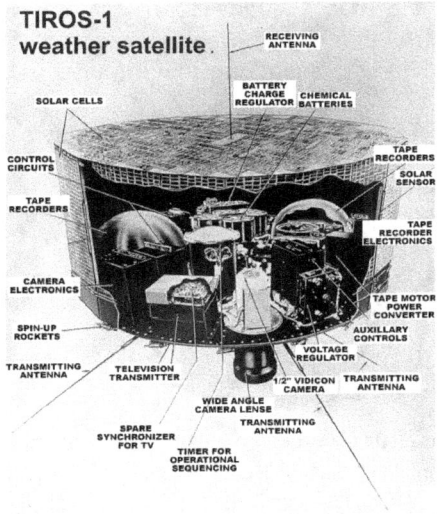

TIROS-1 weather satellite

Wednesday 30: A state of emergency is declared in South Africa after mass protests over the Sharpeville Massacre.

Thursday 31: Several hundred political prisoners, incarcerated since the failed Hungarian uprising against Soviet rule in 1956, are freed as part of an amnesty.

Friday 1: The US launches its first weather satellite, TIROS-1 (Television Infra Red Observation Satellite). The world's first weather report with satellite photos is broadcast the same day.

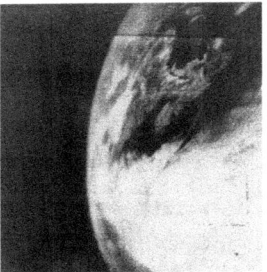

The first TV picture of the Earth, taken by TIROS-1.

Saturday 2: British olympic gold winning runner Linford Christie is born in Saint Andrew Parish, Jamaica.

Sunday 3: The Charismatic Movement begins within mainstream Christianity when an Episcopalian priest, Rev Dennis Bennett of Van Nuys, California, tells his congregation of his Pentecostal experiences.

April 1960

Monday 4: At the 32nd Academy Awards, *Ben Hur* wins a record 11 Oscars, including Best Picture.

Tuesday 5: Peter Llewellyn Davies MC, the inspiration for novelist J.M. Barrie's character Peter Pan, commits suicide aged 63.

Wednesday 6: Britain's Short SC1, the first VTOL (vertical take off and landing) aeroplane, makes a successful test flight.

Marina Berti and Charlton Heston in Ben Hur.

Thursday 7: The African National Congress (ANC) is banned in South Africa, leading to the creation of its guerilla wing led by Nelson Mandela.

Friday 8: Rumours spread that radio signals picked up at the National Radio Astronomy Observatory in West Virginia are from extraterrestrial life-forms. The source is later traced to an aeroplane.

Saturday 9: An unsuccessful assassination attempt is made on South Africa's Prime Minister, Hendrick Verwoerd, by a white farmer, David Pratt, in Johannesburg.

Sunday 10: The last successful U2 high altitude spy-plane flight by the USAF takes place over the Soviet Union.

The Short SC1 aeroplane.

April 1960

Monday 11: Television presenter Jeremy Clarkson (*Top Gear*) is born in Doncaster, England.

Tuesday 12: Eric Peugeot, the four year old grandson of French automotive tycoon Jean-Pierre Peugeot, is kidnapped near Paris. He is returned three days later after payment of a $300,000 ransom.

Wednesday 13: The USA launches Transit I-B, the first successful navigation satellite.

Thursday 14: *Bye Bye Birdie*, starring Dick Van Dyke, the first musical to have rock and roll music as part of its score, opens on Broadway.

Friday 15: Prince Phillipe, later King Phillipe of the Belgians, is born near Laeken, Belgium.

Saturday 16: The breakdown of political relations between the USSR and China, known as the Sino-Soviet Split, worsens as the Chinese communist party accuses the USSR of abandoning Leninism.

Sunday 17: Rock and roll star Eddie Cochrane, author of *Summertime Blues* dies following a car accident the previous day while on tour in Wiltshire, England. Fellow musician Gene Vincent is seriously injured in the crash.

Eddie Cochran's memorial.

April 1960

Monday 18: The Screen Actors Guild, led by future US President Ronald Reagan, ends the strike it began on 7 March.

Tuesday 19: The first x-ray photograph of the sun is taken, using a camera mounted on a Aerobee rocket.

Ronald Reagan.

Wednesday 20: Elvis Presley begins work on the film *GI Blues*, his first picture since being conscripted into the army.

Thursday 21: Following mass defections from East Berlin, East German police cross illegally into West Berlin in an attempt to stop the flow of escapees; two East German police officers are arrested and the remainder retreat.

Friday 22: France's President, Charles de Gaulle, is given an enthusiastic welcome by large crowds during his state visit to Washington, DC.

Memorial to the 'Biloxi Wade-In' protest of 24 April.

Saturday 23: Paranormal researcher Timothy Dinsdale captures what some believe to be the only film footage of the Loch Ness Monster in Scotland. Later expert analysis suggests it is a boat rather than any kind of creature.

Sunday 24: Violence erupts when 100 black protesters march on a whites-only beach in Biloxi, Mississippi. Serious rioting follows the demonstration; the US Department of Justice ends segregated beaches a month later.

April/May 1960

Monday 25: The nuclear submarine USS *Triton* completes the first underwater circumnavigation of the globe.

Tuesday 26: Syngman Rhee, President of South Korea, resigns and flees the country after a week-long uprising in which 145 people are killed.

Wednesday 27: A referendum held in Ghana decides that the country will change from a constitutional monarchy under Queen Elizabeth II to a republic within the British Commonwealth.

Thursday 28: Scottish crime novelist Ian Rankin OBE is born in Cardenden, Fife.

Friday 29: Golfer Bill Glasson is born in Fresno, California.

Saturday 30: David Miscavige, leader of the Church of Scientology, is born in Philadelphia, PA.

Sunday 1: USAF U2 spy plane pilot Gary Powers is shot down over the Soviet Union and is captured by Soviet forces after parachuting to safety from 70,500 ft (21,488m). He is sentenced to ten years' imprisonment but released in 1962.

Below: Gary Powers and a U2 spyplane in flight.

May 1960

Monday 2: Dr Robert H. Goetz of the Van Etten Hospital in New York City performs the first coronary artery bypass operation.

Tuesday 3: As part of a civil defence drill, at 2.00pm EDT, all radio and TV broadcasting is stopped in the USA for 30 minutes and air raid sirens are sounded, with all citizens ordered to proceed to their nearest air raid shelter.

Wednesday 4: Comedienne Lucille Ball is granted a divorce from on-screen and real-life husband Desi Arnaz.

Thursday 5: In the Soviet Parliament, Premier Nikita Kruschev announces the downing of Gary Powers' U2 spy plane.

Friday 6: In a ceremony at Westminster Abbey, HRH Princess Margaret, sister of HM Queen Elizabeth II, marries Antony Armstrong-Jones, Earl of Snowdon.

Kruschev.

Saturday 7: In the FA Cup Final at Wembley Stadium, London, Wolverhampton Wanderers defeat Blackburn Rovers 3-0.

Sunday 8: Cuba and the Soviet Union formally re-establish diplomatic relations, which were severed in 1952.

ISSUED UNDER THE AUTHORITY OF THE MINISTER OF WORKS

THE MARRIAGE OF HER ROYAL HIGHNESS

Princess Margaret

WITH

Mr Antony Armstrong-Jones

FRIDAY 6 MAY 1960 HORSE GUARDS PARADE

ADMIT ONE | BLOCK M ROW C SEAT 13

PLEASE SEE REVERSE

Left: ticket for the Royal Wedding of Princess Margaret and Antony Armstrong-Jones.

May 1960

Monday 9: The US Food and Drug Administration approves the first oral birth control pill, Enovid.

Tuesday 10: The submarine USS *Triton* returns to the USA after completing the first underwater circumnavigation of the globe on 25 April.

Wednesday 11: Israeli secret service agents kidnap prominent Nazi Adolf Eichmann in Buenos Aires, where he is held captive until being flown to Israel to stand trial for war crimes.

Adolf Eichmann in 1942.

Thursday 12: Soviet Premier Kruschev warns that if the US makes any further spy plane flights over Soviet territory, 'this might lead to war'.

Friday 13: The launch of the USA's Echo 1 communications satellite ends in failure.

Saturday 14: US President Eisenhower flies to Paris for the 'Four Power' summit meeting between the USA, UK, France and the Soviet Union.

Model of the Vostok rocket.

Sunday 15: The Soviet Union launches Sputnik IV, a mock-up of a manned Vostok rocket using a dummy instead of a pilot. The craft fails to return to Earth until September 1962, where part of it crash-lands on Manitowoc, Wisconsin, USA.

May 1960

Monday 16: Shortly after the beginning of the Four Power summit in Paris, Soviet Premier Nikita Kruschev walks out following a rant in which he cancels his previous invitation to US President Eisenhower for a Soviet tour.

Tuesday 17: Joseph 'Mad Dog' Taborsky goes to the electric chair in Connecticut for a series of brutal murders in the 1950s.

Wednesday 18: The last episode of long-running US drama series *Playhouse 90* is broadcast on CBS-TV.

Thursday 19: 17,000 people attend the largest American anti-nuclear rally up to this date, which takes place at Madison Square Garden in New York City; speakers include former First Lady Eleanor Roosevelt.

Friday 20: The Beatles (then known as the 'Silver Beetles') make one of their earliest public performances, as the backing band for singer Johnny Gentle at the town hall in Alloa, Scotland.

Saturday 21: Private Buzo Minagawa of the Imperial Japanese Army is discovered in a jungle on the Pacific island of Guam, refusing to believe that Japan surrendered 15 years earlier.

Sunday 22: Nearly 5,000 people are killed when a 9.5 earthquake hits Valdivia in Chile *(below)*, in what is said to be the largest earthquake of the twentieth century.

May 1960

Monday 23: Another Japanese soldier, Masashi Ito, is discovered on the island of Guam. He and Pte Minagawa, discovered two days earlier, are returned to Japan.

Tuesday 24: Actress Kristin Scott Thomas (*Four Weddings and a Funeral, The English Patient*) is born in Cornwall, England.

Wednesday 25: Four more earthquakes hit Chile, resulting in another 5,000 deaths.

Thursday 26: US Ambassador Henry Cabot Lodge reveals to the United Nations in New York that a Soviet bug has been found in a replica of the Great Seal of the United States presented as a gift to the US Embassy in Moscow.

Kristin Scott Thomas.

Friday 27: Ireland's Grand Canal, connecting Dublin and Limerick, closes after 156 years in operation.

Saturday 28: The Broadway musical *Greenwillow* starring Anthony Perkins closes after 95 performances.

Sunday 29: Britain's Stirling Moss wins the Monaco Grand Prix motor race.

Above: replica of the Great Seal and right, the bug hidden inside.

May/June 1960

Monday 30: Boris Pasternak, author of Dr Zhivago, dies aged 70.

Tuesday 31: At a Democratic dinner in Los Angeles, Senator John F Kennedy makes a speech about the growing U2 spy plane crisis, stating that the USA must not 'respond to the new Russian threat with weakness and appeasement'.

Wednesday 1: Television broadcasting begins in New Zealand as the Adventures of Robin Hood is transmitted on NZTV.

Thursday 2: John Lennon, Paul McCartney, Stuart Sutcliffe and Tommy Moore perform for the first time under the name 'The Beatles', at the civic hall in Neston, Cheshire, England.

Friday 3: Argentina demands that Israel returns Nazi fugitive Adolf Eichmann, kidnapped by Mossad agents on 11 May, and asks for reparations for infringed sovereignty.

Saturday 4: France amends its constitution to allow former colonial possessions to remain in the French Community, the equivalent of Britain's Commonwealth.

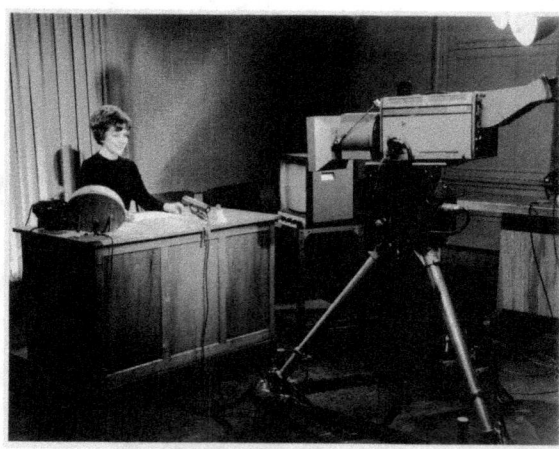

Sunday 5: Dwight D Eisenhower becomes the first in a long line of Presidents to make the inaugural speech at the University of Notre Dame in Indiana.

An early NZTV broadcast.

June 1960

Monday 6: 18 year old singer Barbara Streisand gives her first paid public performance, winning a talent contest in Greenwich Village, New York City.

Tuesday 7: A missile and nuclear warhead catch fire in McGuire Airforce Base in New Jersey; there is no risk of explosion but a plutonium leak occurs.

Left: Barbara Streisand.

Wednesday 8: Singer Mick Hucknall of Simply Red is born in Denton near Manchester, England.

Thursday 9: Typhoon Mary hits Hong Kong and mainland China, killing over 1600 people.

Friday 10: 29 people are killed in Australia's worst peacetime air crash in the sea off Mackay, Queensland; on the same day 31 people die when an Aeroflot aeroplane crashes in Georgia, USSR.

Mick Hucknall.

Saturday 11: The operatic version of Shakespeare's *A Midsummer Night's Dream*, with music by Peter Pears and Benjamin Britten, premieres at the Aldeburgh Festival in Suffolk, England.

Sunday 12: Typhoon Mary finally dies down after causing major destruction across the Far East.

June 1960

Monday 13: A Japanese submarine sunk in Pearl Harbor on 7 December 1941 is raised by the USS *Current* and returned to Japan.

Tuesday 14: 14 people are killed when a Pacific Northern Airlines plane crashes on Mount Gilbert, Alaska.

Wednesday 15: Thousands of protestors, angry about Japan's recent security pact with the USA, storm the parliament building in Tokyo; one person is killed and 600 injured.

Thursday 16: *Psycho*, directed by Alfred Hitchcock and starring Anthony Perkins and Janet Leigh premieres in New York City.

Friday 17: Baseball player Ted Williams of the Boston Red Socks hits his 500th home run, the fourth player to reach the milestone in the history of the game.

Poster for Hitchcock's *Psycho*.

Saturday 18: The Middleton Railway in Leeds, England, becomes the first standard-gauge railway to be run entirely by volunteers.

Sunday 19: Three racing drivers are killed on the same day; America's Jimmy Bryan at Langhorne Speedway in Pennsylvania, and Britain's Chris Bristow and Alan Stacey during the Belgian Grand Prix.

June 1960

Monday 20: Nan Winton makes her debut as the first female newsreader on BBC television.

Tuesday 21: The last USAF B-29 bomber, dating from the Second World War, is taken out of operational service.

Wednesday 22: 11 people are killed in a fire at Henderson's department store in Church Street, Liverpool, England. The store had no fire alarm and no fire drill; the disaster leads to a tightening up of fire safety law in Britain.

Thursday 23: Enovid, the first oral contraceptive drug, becomes available for sale across the USA.

Friday 24: Two bystanders are killed during an unsuccessful assassination attempt on Romulo Betancourt, President of Venezuela.

Saturday 25: Talks begin between the French government and the FLN, the separatist group of France's north African colony of Algeria.

Sunday 26: The east African colony of British Somaliland is granted independence by Britain, and combines with the former Italian Somaliland to form the Somali Republic.

The last B-29 bomber is taken out of operational service. As of 2019, only two airworthy examples remain.

June/July 1960

Monday 27: 104 people are killed as Typhoon Olive strikes the Phillippines.

Tuesday 28: 45 miners are killed in an explosion at Six Bells Colliery, Monmouthshire, Wales.

Wednesday 29: The state of the art new BBC Television Centre opens in Shepherd's Bush, west London.

Thursday 30: Lionel Bart's musical *Oliver!*, based on Charles Dickens' novel *Oliver Twist*, premieres in London.

Lionel Bart.

Friday 1: The Belgian Congo is proclaimed independent from Belgian rule; the liberation is followed by an army mutiny and civil war.

Saturday 2: Fighting breaks out among 3000 people at the Newport Jazz Festival in Newport, Rhode Island, over seating allocation; National Guard soldiers are required to restore order.

Sunday 3: Britain's Jack Brabham wins the French Grand Prix at Reims-Gueux.

Jack Brabham.

July 1960

Monday 4: The first fifty-star flags of the USA are raised, following the accession of Alaska and Hawaii to the Union in 1959. This replaces the 48-star flag introduced in 1912 when Arizona and New Mexico joined the Union.

Tuesday 5: Violence erupts in the Congo; European settlers are attacked following an army mutiny.

Wednesday 6: Aneurin Bevan, former British Minister of Health (1945-1951) and architect of the National Health Service system of state medical insurance, dies aged 62.

Thursday 7: Italian police shoot dead five people during a Communist demonstration in the city of Reggio Emilia.

Aneurin Bevan, architect of Britain's National Health Service.

Friday 8: Following the nationalisation of sports teams under the Castro regime, Cuba's international baseball team, the Havana Sugar Kings, moves to Jersey City, New Jersey.

Saturday 9: During a boating accident, Rodger Woodward, aged 7, becomes the first person known to have survived being accidentally swept across the Niagra Falls. Master Woodward falls 165 feet but only sustains minor injuries.

Sunday 10: The Soviet Union beats Yugoslavia 2-1 to win the first UEFA European Football Championship, held in Paris, France.

July 1960

Monday 11: Harper Lee's Pulitzer Prize winning novel of the USA's deep south, *To Kill a Mockingbird*, is published.

Tuesday 12: The Etch-a-Sketch drawing machine, invented by Andre Cassagnes, goes on sale for the first time.

The Etch-a-Sketch. It goes on to become one of the best-selling toys of all time.

Wednesday 13: An unsuccessful assassination attempt is made on Nobosuke Kishi, Prime Minister of Japan.

Thursday 14: Lyndon B Johnson announces he will stand as Vice-President nominee with John F Kennedy in the forthcoming US Presidential elections.

Friday 15: Nobosuke Kishi resigns as Prime Minister of Japan.

Saturday 16: The split between China and the Soviet Union is completed, as the USSR announces the cancellation of all joint projects and the removal of all Soviet advisors from China.

Sunday 17: Joseph Kasavabu, President of the newly independent Republic of Congo, threatens to invite the Soviet Union to send troops to intervene if Belgian troops are not withdrawn.

Monday 18: *I'm Sorry* by fifteen year old singer Brenda Lee hits the top of the US Billboard Hot 100 charts.

Tuesday 19: 39 Belgian Air Force personnel are killed when their plane hits a mountain near Gomo in the Republic of Congo.

Wednesday 20: Sirimavo Bandaranaike of Ceylon (now Sri Lanka) becomes the world's first woman Prime Minister.

Sirimavo Bandaranaike.

Thursday 21: The first television station in Egypt begins broadcasting, with verses from the Koran followed by an address by President Nasser.

Jean Lesage, Premier of Quebec.

Friday 22: The 'Quiet Revolution' of social and economic reforms in the Canadian province of Quebec begins, as Jean Lesage takes over as Premier.

Saturday 23: Betsy Rawls wins the US Women's Open golf championship at Worcester, Massachusetts.

Sunday 24: Marshal Ivan Konev retires as chief of the Warsaw Pact, the military alliance of communist countries. He is replaced by Marshal Andre Grechko.

July 1960

Monday 25: The colour bar is ended at the Woolworth's lunch counter in Greensboro, North Carolina, following highly publicised protests which began in January.

Tuesday 26: The Soviet Union agrees to US proposals for each country to inspect the other's missile sites annually; the proposals are not carried out until over 25 years later.

Wednesday 27: The Republic of Ireland ends its policy of neutrality as it sends troops to the Congo as part of the UN peacekeeping mission.

Thursday 28: The Royal Navy conducts 'Operation Shop Window', a large-scale demonstration of re-fueling aircraft carriers at sea, off the coast of southern England near Portsmouth.

Friday 29: The USA launches Mercury-Atlas 1, a test rocket for a future manned space mission; it fails after 58 seconds and crash lands in the ocean.

Saturday 30: South and North Korean forces engage for the first time since the end of the Korean War in 1953, as a North Korean gunboat is sunk near Kojin.

Sunday 31: The Malayan Emergency is officially declared over. Over 1800 British and Commonwealth troops and police were killed in the 12-year operation against communist guerillas.

The Mercury-Atlas 1 rocket at lift-off.

August 1960

Monday 1: The Republic of Dahomey becomes independent of French West Africa. It is later renamed Benin.

Tuesday 2: Proposals for a third US baseball league, the Continental League, are abandoned following a meeting between the National and American leagues.

Wednesday 3: The Republic of Niger, formerly part of French West Africa, becomes independent.

Thursday 4: NASA test pilot Joseph A Walker sets a world speed record when he flies an X-15 aeroplane at 2,196 mph.

Chubby Checker.

Friday 5: The Republic of Upper Volta, formerly part of French West Africa, becomes independent; it is later renamed Burkina Faso.

Saturday 6: Singer Chubby Checker starts a nationwide US dance craze when he performs his song *The Twist* on the TV show Dick Clark's American Bandstand.

Sunday 7: The Ivory Coast (Cote d'Ivoire) becomes independent of France.

World air speed record holder Joseph A Walker with his X-15.

August 1960

Monday 8: The song *Itsy Bitsy Teeny Weenie Yellow Polka Dot Bikini* by Brian Hyland hits number one in the USA.

Tuesday 9: The government of Laos is overthrown in a military coup led by Captain Kong Le.

Wednesday 10: Spanish actor Antonio Banderas (*Zorro, Shrek*) is born in Malaga, Spain.

Thursday 11: The Republic of Chad, formerly part of French Equatorial Africa, becomes independent of France.

Friday 12: The USA launches Echo 1, the first communications satellite. A pre-recorded message from President Eisenhower is transmitted from California to New Jersey via the satellite.

Saturday 13: The Central African Republic, formerly part of French Equatorial Africa, becomes independent from France under President David Dacko.

Sunday 14: Singer Sarah Brightman born in Berkhamsted, Hertfordshire, England.

The Echo 1 satellite's 100ft diameter balloon was designed to inflate in the upper atmosphere. The similar Echo 2 satellite is shown left undergoing tests.

August 1960

Monday 15: The former French Congo becomes independent, confusingly renaming itself as the Republic of Congo, exactly the same name as the former Belgian Congo. To distinguish between the two capitals, the former French capital is named Congo (Brazzaville) and the former Belgian capital is named Congo (Leopoldville).

Tuesday 16: Joseph Kittinger sets a new world record for the highest ever parachute jump, from a balloon 102,800 feet (19.46 miles) above New Mexico. On the same day, Cyprus is granted independence by Great Britain.

Wednesday 17: American actor Sean Penn is born in Santa Monica, California.

Thursday 18: The first photograph from a spy satellite is taken, showing a Soviet airfield. The satellite is able to take more pictures than all of the previous U2 spyplane flights put together.

Kittinger makes his record jump.

Friday 19: The Soviet Union launches Sputnik 5, containing two dogs (Belka and Strelka), 40 mice, 2 rats and several plants; all are returned safely to Earth the next day.

Saturday 20: Senegal secedes from the short-lived Mali Federation of two former French colonies in Africa; the remainder retains its name of Mali.

Sunday 21: The USS *Seadragon* completes the first underwater crossing of the Northwest Passage, the Arctic sea route between the Atlantic and Pacific Oceans.

August 1960

Monday 22: Discussions in Geneva on a nuclear test ban treaty between the US, USSR and UK are adjourned indefinitely.

Tuesday 23: American songwriter Oscar Hammerstein II dies aged 65.

Wednesday 24: The coldest ever temperature on Earth (-88.3C/-126.9F) is recorded at the Soviet Vostok station in Antarctica; it is not surpassed until 1983.

Oscar Hammerstein.

Thursday 25: The 1960 Olympics opens in Rome, with runner Giancarlo Peris lighting the Olympic Flame.

Friday 26: Danish cyclist Knud Enemark Jensen dies aged 23 following an accident in an Olympic cycling event; postmortem tests reveal he was under the influence of performance-enhancing drugs at the time.

Saturday 27: British swimmer Anita Lonsbrough breaks the world record for the 200 metres race at the Olympics, with a time of 2.49.5.

Sunday 28: The United Nations announces that it has posted sufficient numbers of troops in the Congo to keep order, and demands that the last of Belgium's forces be withdrawn.

Giancarlo Peris with the Olympic torch.

August/Sept 1960

Monday 29: The Prime Minister of Jordan, Hazza Majali, is assassinated by a bomb attack on his office in Amman.

Tuesday 30: The US women's relay swimming team beats Australia to win the gold medal at the Rome olympics.

Wednesday 31: The USA's Bill Nieder wins an Olympic gold medal for a shot putt throw of 19.68m (64.5ft). Nieder was also the first athlete to throw a shot putt over 60 feet while still in high school.

Thursday 1: The lights of Broadway are turned off for one minute and the lights of London's Theatreland dimmed in honour of songwriter Oscar Hammerstein II, who died on 23 August.

Friday 2: American Ralph Boston breaks the Olympic long jump record (set in 1936 by Jesse Owens) by completing a jump of 26 feet 7.75 inches.

Dawn Fraser of the Australian Olympic ladies' swimming team poses by the pool.

Saturday 3: More than 300 people are killed as Congolese troops engage rebel forces in the Mining State of South Kasai, which broke away from the Republic of Congo on 8 August.

Sunday 4: The USA's Phil Hill wins the 1960 Italian Grand Prix motor race at Monza, Italy.

September 1960

Monday 5: The USA's Cassius Clay (later Muhammed Ali) defeats Poland's Zbigniew Pietrzykowski to win a gold medal in the Olympic light heavyweight boxing competition.

Tuesday 6: Moscow announces that two American National Security Agency cryptologists missing since 24 June, William Martin and Bernon Mitchell, have defected to the USSR.

Wednesday 7: Crown Prince Constantine II of Greece wins a gold medal for sailing in the Olympics, competing in his yacht the Nirefs at Naples, Italy.

Thursday 8: Richardson-Merrell pharmaceuticals submits its application to sell Thalidomide, the morning sickness pill which is later found to cause serious birth defects.

Hugh Grant.

Friday 9: Actor Hugh Grant *(Four Weddings and a Funeral, Notting Hill, Love Actually)* is born in London, England.

Saturday 10: Abebe Bikila of Ethiopia wins the Olympic marathon, setting a world record of 2.15.16.2. Mr Bikila, the first sub-Saharan African to win an Olympic gold medal, also runs the entire race barefoot.

Sunday 11: The 1960 Rome Olympics closes.

Abebe Bikila wins the Olympic marathon.

September 1960

Monday 12: US Presidential candidate John F Kennedy, a Roman Catholic, addresses a gathering of Protestant clergy in Houston, Texas, allaying their concerns about a Roman Catholic holding the office of President. Kennedy announces 'I am not the Catholic candidate for President. I am the Democratic Party's candidate for president who happens also to be a Catholic'.

Tuesday 13: A total eclipse of the moon takes place, visible over much of the Pacific Ocean.

Wednesday 14: The Organisation of Petroleum Exporting Countries (OPEC) comprising Iran, Iraq, Kuwait, Saudi Arabia and Venezuela is formed in Baghdad.

Thursday 15: The government of Cuba nationalises cigar production, seizing 16 cigar factories.

Friday 16: Amos Alonzo Stagg, assistant football coach at Stockton College, California, retires aged 98 as one of the longest serving college football coaches on record, having started his career in 1890. He also played in the first public basketball game following the sport's invention in 1892.

Amos Stagg in 1906.

Saturday 17: British racing driver Damon Hill is born in London.

Sunday 18: Alfred John Evans, England test cricketer and author of the First World War POW book *The Escaping Club*, dies aged 71.

Damon Hill.

September 1960

Monday 19: Soviet premier Nikita Kruschev along with other communist bloc leaders arrives in New York for the opening of the United Nations General Assembly; he is greeted with a mixture of cheers and boos by crowds at the airport.

Tuesday 20: Soviet premier Nikita Kruschev meets Cuban leader Fidel Castro for the first time while both attend the UN General Assembly.

Wednesday 21: Drs Albert Starr and Dwight Harken perform the first implantation of an artificial mitral heart valve, known as the Starr-Edwards valve, on Philip Amundsen (52) at the University of Oregon. Mr Amundsen survives for ten years after the operation.

Thursday 22: The Federation of Mali achieves full independence from France and becomes the Republic of Mali.

Howdy Doody.

Friday 23: At the United Nations General Assembly in New York, Soviet premier Nikita Kruschev calls for the Assembly to be replaced by a three member panel representing the western nations, the communists and the non-aligned 'third world'.

Saturday 24: The final episode of long running US children's puppet show, *Howdy Doody*, airs on NBC TV. Presented by Buffalo Bob Smith, it ran for 2343 episodes from 1947.

Sunday 25: Novelist and etiquette manual writer Emily Post dies in New York City aged 87.

September/Oct 1960

Monday 26: US Presidential candidates John F Kennedy (Democrat) and Richard M Nixon (Republican) take part in the first televised pre-election debate. An Act of Congress was required for the broadcast to take place without involving other parties' nominees.

Tuesday 27: Womens' suffrage campaigner Estelle Pankhurst, daughter of Emmeline Pankhurst, dies aged 78.

Wednesday 28: US singer Jennifer Rush (*The Power of Love*) is born in New York City.

Kennedy and Nixon on TV.

Thursday 29: At the United Nations General Assembly in New York, Soviet premier Nikita Kruschev angrily interrupts British Prime Minister Harold Macmillan, who politely pauses to allow him to finish his rant.

Friday 30: Animated comedy series *The Flintstones* is broadcast on US TV for the first time.

Saturday 1: The British colony of Nigeria becomes an independent Commonwealth country, with Governor General Nnamdi Azikiwe representing its head of state, Queen Elizabeth II.

Jennifer Rush.

Sunday 2: The antibiotic resistant form of bacteria known as MRSA is first identified, by Dr M Patricia Jevons at the Staphylococcus Reference Laboratory in Colindale, London.

October 1960

Monday 3: Dwight D Eisenhower becomes the oldest President of the United States; at 69 years 354 days he is older than the previous record reached by Andrew Jackson in 1837.

Tuesday 4: 62 people are killed when an airliner crashes after being struck by birds near Boston, Massachusetts.

Wednesday 5: South Africans vote in a referendum to become a republic within the British Commonwealth; President C R Swart replaces Queen Elizabeth II as head of state.

C R Swart becomes President of South Africa.

Thursday 6: *Spartacus*, directed by Stanley Kubrick and starring Kirk Douglas, premieres in New York City. It goes on to become the top-grossing film of the year.

Friday 7: The CIA prepares a box of poisoned cigars as part of an assassination plot against Cuba's leader Fidel Castro. The cigars are delivered to an agent in Cuba in February 1961 but never used.

Saturday 8: The 30 mile long range of the Queen Fabiola Mountains in the Antarctic is discovered by the Belgian Antarctic Expedition.

Kirk Douglas: star of *Spartacus*.

Sunday 9: The first 92 National Historic Landmarks are designated by the National Parks Service in the USA. The first is the Sergeant Floyd Monument in Sioux City, Iowa.

October 1960

Monday 10: The first Soviet Molniya rocket bearing a probe aimed at Mars, fails five minutes after launching.

Tuesday 11: Actor Richard Cromwell, who starred with Bette Davis in *Jezebel* and was married to future *Murder She Wrote* star Angela Lansbury, dies aged 50.

Wednesday 12: In a now-legendary incident said to have occurred during the United Nations General Assembly in New York, Soviet premier Nikita Kruschev removes his shoe and bangs it on his desk to interrupt a speech by Phillippines delegate Lorenzo Sumolong.

Thursday 13: The third Presidential debate between candidates John F Kennedy and Richard M Nixon is broadcast on US TV.

Friday 14: The 11th General Conference on Weights and Measures redefines the metre; previously it was based on a metal bar held in secure storage since 1889. The new definition is optical: 1,650,763.73 wavelengths of the orange-red line of Krypton-86.

The metal metre bar, introduced in 1889.

Saturday 15: British Olympic gold runner Steve Cram, the first man to run 1500m in under 3.30, is born in Gateshead, County Durham.

Sunday 16: 277 insurgents and 40 French soldiers are killed in fierce fighting in the north African colony of Algeria.

October 1960

Monday 17: Over 3000 people are killed in East Pakistan (now Bangladesh) during floods caused by a cyclone.

Tuesday 18: Belgian martial arts expert and film star Jean Claude Van Damme is born near Brussels, Belgium.

Wednesday 19: The US government announces an embargo on all American exports to Cuba, except for medicine and food.

Jean Claude Van Damme.

Thursday 20: The price of gold rises sharply in London following fears that the USA is about to devalue its currency; the Americans respond by increasing the gold supply to the Bank of England.

Friday 21: Britain has two military firsts on this day: HM Queen Elizabeth II launches the country's first nuclear submarine, HMS *Dreadnought*, and the prototype VTOL (Vertical Take Off and Landing) Harrier Jump Jet makes its maiden flight.

Saturday 22: Republican vice-president nominee Henry Cabot Lodge predicts that the Cold War could last until 1985. In fact, it lasts until 1991.

The Hawker P1127, the prototype Harrier jump jet.

Sunday 23: A woman throws a drink over Democrat Presidential nominee John F Kennedy while he is driving in an open car in Milwaukee. Kennedy is unhurt and no charges are made.

October 1960

Monday 24: In the Nedelin Catastrophe, the USSR's Field Marshall Nedelin and 100 others are killed when a missile explodes on the launchpad during tests at Baikonur Cosmodrome. Nedelin had ordered repairs to be made on the missile without removing the fuel. His death is covered up and the incident is not made public until 1989.

Tuesday 25: The first fully electronic battery powered wristwatch, the Accutron 214, is revealed to the public, with a price tag of $175 (around $1500 in 2019 money).

Wednesday 26: Jose Maria Lemus, President of El Salvador, is ousted in a bloodless coup and replaced by a joint military and civil junta.

Thursday 27: Eggs and tomatoes are thrown at Republican presidential candidate Richard M Nixon during campaigning in Michigan.

Friday 28: The new procedure of microsurgery is brought to the public's attention at a gathering of the American Heart Association in St Louis, Missouri. Its pioneers, Drs Julius H Jacobson II, Ernesto L Suarez and Donald B Miller describe a successful experiment to reconnect a dog's blood vessels.

Cassius Clay (Muhammed Ali).

Saturday 29: Cassius Clay (later Muhammed Ali) makes his professional boxing debut (previous bouts were under amateur status) defeating Tunney Hunsaker in Louisville, Kentucky.

Sunday 30: Michael Woodruff performs the first successful kidney transplant operation in the United Kingdom, at the Edinburgh Royal Infirmary.

October/Nov 1960

Monday 31: At least 10,000 are thought to have died when a cyclone hits East Pakistan (now Bangladesh), causing flooding which submerges several islands.

Tuesday 1: Britain's Prime Minister Harold Macmillan announces that US nuclear submarines will be based in British waters on the Firth of Clyde in Scotland.

Wednesday 2: In a landmark decision, a jury in London concludes that DH Lawrence's book *Lady Chatterley's Lover*, banned since the 1920s, does not breach British obscenity laws. The case is often seen as a precursor to the more relaxed moral standards of the 1960s.

Thursday 3: The USA's Explorer 8 satellite is launched to monitor the Earth's ionosphere; it later confirms the existence of a helium layer in the upper atmosphere.

Cover of the Penguin Books edition of *Lady Chatterley's Lover*.

Friday 4: During a rally for presidential nominee John F Kennedy in Chicago, Jaime Cruz Alejandro is arrested after forcing his way through crowds to Mr Kennedy's open car while carrying a .25 calibre pistol. Alejandro is later released without charge. This is the second recent attempted assault on Mr Kennedy, who is assassinated in an open car in Dallas in 1963.

Saturday 5: Mack Sennett, silent film director and actor best known for his Keystone Kops comedy movies, dies aged 80.

Sunday 6: One person is killed and 18 are injured when a bomb explodes on a subway car in New York City, the first to claim a life in a series of five bomb attacks on the city since 2 October.

November 1960

Monday 7: Presidential candidate Richard M Nixon appears in the first telethon in the history of election campaigning, taking part in a live phone-in broadcast simultaneously on ABC, CBS and NBC.

Tuesday 8: In the Presidential election, US voters cast the closest popular vote in the country's history. John F Kennedy wins by a margin of 1/6 of one percent of votes cast.

Wednesday 9: The US navy is sent to Nicaragua following insurgency attacks on the Costa Rican border.

John F Kennedy casts his vote at the polling station in Boston Public Library.

Thursday 10: The first copies of *Lady Chatterley's Lover,* published by Penguin Books following a legal ruling that it is not obscene, go on sale in England and Wales. It becomes an instant bestseller.

Friday 11: RMS *Britannic*, the last of the great White Star Line ocean liners makes its final voyage from Liverpool to New York City.

Saturday 12: The first Soviet nuclear submarine, K-19, is completed.

Sunday 13: Singer and actor Sammy Davis Jr marries Swedish actress May Britt (above).

November 1960

Monday 14: Ruby Bridges *(above)*, escorted by police officers for her own safety, becomes the first black pupil to enroll at the formerly segregated William Frantz Elementary School in New Orleans. The racially charged incident is captured by artist Norman Rockwell in his painting *The Problem We All Live With*.

Tuesday 15: The USA's first nuclear submarine, the USS *George Washington* is launched, armed with 16 Polaris missiles.

Wednesday 16: Film star Clark Gable dies aged 59, a few days after filming *The Misfits* with Marilyn Monroe.

Thursday 17: British TV and radio presenter Jonathan Ross is born in London.

Friday 18: Singer Kim Wilde, the daughter of singers Marty Wilde and Joyce Baker, is born in London.

Saturday 19: German electronic specialist and radar pioneer Hans Erich Hollmann dies aged 61.

Sunday 20: Hayato Ikeda's Liberal Democratic Party is victorious in Japan's election.

November 1960

Monday 21: UN troops engage the Congolese army for the first time since the Congo crisis began. A force of 150 Tunisian soldiers fight for three hours to defend the Ghanaian embassy against an attack.

Tuesday 22: The USS *Ethan Allen* is launched. At 410 feet in length it is the longest nuclear submarine in the US Navy.

Wednesday 23: The world's second weather satellite, TIROS-2 is launched. It is equipped with altitude control systems that enable it to remain almost stationary over north America.

Thursday 24: In basketball, Wilt Chamberlain of the Philadelphia Warriors sets a record of 55 rebounds in a game; a total unsurpassed for over 50 years.

Friday 25: The last of the USA's daytime radio soap operas, *Young Dr Malone, Right to Happiness, The Second Mrs Burton* and *Ma Perkins* are all brought to an end, as audiences increasingly move to TV dramas.

Saturday 26: Keith Holyoake's National Party is victorious in New Zealand's elections; Mr Holyoake becomes Prime Minister on 12 December, serving in that role until 1972.

Keith Holyoake.

Sunday 27: Former England cricket captain Fred Fane MC dies aged 85. He was the first Irishman to score a century in test cricket.

November/Dec 1960

Monday 28: *Are You Lonesome Tonight* by Elvis Presley hits number one in the USA.

Tuesday 29: The Soviet Union's anti-ballistic missile, the V-1000, is successfully tested at Sary Shagan.

Wednesday 30: English footballer and commentator Gary Lineker is born in Leicester.

Gary Lineker.

Thursday 1: The Soviets launch Sputnik 6, a rocket containing two dogs plus mice, insects and plants; re-entry is unsuccessful and the capsule burns up in the Earth's atmosphere.

Friday 2: The Archbishop of Canterbury, Geoffrey Fisher, meets Pope John Paul XXIII in the Vatican. It is the first such meeting between holders of those offices since 1397.

Saturday 3: The most expensive theatrical production to this date, *Camelot*, opens on Broadway, starring Richard Burton as King Arthur and Julie Andrews as Lady Guinevere.

Sunday 4: Mauritania's application to become the 100th member of the United Nations is vetoed by the Soviet Union on the grounds that Mongolia's application had been rejected.

Julie Andrews and Richard Burton in *Camelot*.

December 1960

Monday 5: In the US Supreme Court, the case of Boynton *v* Virginia rules that racial segregation in bus stations is unconstitutional.

Tuesday 6: The 9.5 million acre Arctic National Wildlife Refuge is established in Alaska.

The QH-50 DASH in operation.

Wednesday 7: The QH-50 DASH, an early form of drone built to attack submarines, is successfully tested in the USA.

Thursday 8: Hayato Ikeda becomes Prime Minister of Japan.

Friday 9: The first episode of British TV soap opera *Coronation Street* is broadcast. Still on the air in 2019, the show features original cast member Ken Barlow (William Roache, left), the longest serving actor in TV soap history.

Saturday 10: Shakespearian actor Kenneth Branagh (*Henry V, Fortunes of War, Wallander*) is born in Belfast.

Sunday 11: Richard Paul Pavlick drives to the home of John F Kennedy in a car loaded with dynamite, intending to assassinate the President-Elect. He changes his mind and drives off but is arrested four days later and committed to a secure institution.

December 1960

Monday 12: Representatives of the British government announce in the House of Commons that military transport is on stand-by in the event that the 60 British nationals in the war-torn Congo require evacuation.

A3J Vigilante.

Tuesday 13: USAF Commander Leroy A Heath and Lt Henry L Monroe set a new altitude record when they fly their A3J Vigilante to a height of 91,450.8 ft (27, 874m).

Wednesday 14: The first tie in the history of Test Cricket occurs, as the West Indies and Australia end a match in Brisbane with 737 runs each.

Thursday 15: King Mahendra of Nepal deposes his elected government after a 19 month experiment in constitutional monarchy.

Friday 16: 136 people are killed when two airliners collide over New York City; eight fatalities are caused when one of the planes crashes in Brooklyn; the other lands in an unpopulated part of Staten Island.

Saturday 17: 52 people are killed when a US air force plane crash lands in Munich, West Germany.

Sunday 18: The National Museum of India opens in New Delhi.

December 1960

Kennedy bumper sticker.

Monday 19: Following his victory in the popular vote, John F. Kennedy is elected the 35th President of the United States by the Electoral College.

Tuesday 20: The Communist guerilla organisation the National Liberation Front (the 'Viet Cong') is formed in South Vietnam.

Wednesday 21: Major Richard Baer, former commandant of the Auschwitz concentration camp, is arrested after being discovered working as a gardener on the estate of Otto Von Bismarck.

Thursday 22: British architect Sir Ninian Comper, famous for his Victorian Gothic revival style, dies aged 96.

Carole Vorderman.

Friday 23: Following the news that Israel is building a nuclear bomb, President Nasser of Egypt warns that his country will send troops to destroy the bomb-making facility.

Saturday 24: British TV presenter Carol Vorderman (*Countdown*) is born in Bedford, England.

Sunday 25: An earthquake measuring 5.2 on the Richter scale occurs in Victoria, Australia.

December 1960

Monday 26: In American football, the Philadelphia Eagles defeat the Green Bay Packers 17-13 to win the 1960 NFL Championship.

Tuesday 27: A relatively unknown band, The Beatles, receives an ecstatic response from concert-goers during a performance at Litherland Town Hall in Liverpool. The show seals their reputation and starts them on the road to fame.

Wednesday 28: Rebels in the Congo attack a train carrying civilians, many of them women and children. At least 20 people are killed as UN soldiers on board are outnumbered.

Thursday 29: A US Defense Department employee, Arthur Rogers Roddey, is arrested by the FBI after taking almost 200 secret documents on weaponry from the Pentagon.

Friday 30: Angelo Donati, Italian banker and diplomat who saved thousands of French Jews from extermination in the Second World War, dies aged 75.

Saturday 31: Military conscription (National Service) for men aged 17-21 ends in the UK. The last conscripts leave the forces in May 1963.

UN troops in the Congo.

Birthday Notebooks
...a great alternative to a card.

Handy 60 page ruled notebooks with a significant event from the year heading each page.

Available from Montpelier Publishing at Amazon.